Too Little

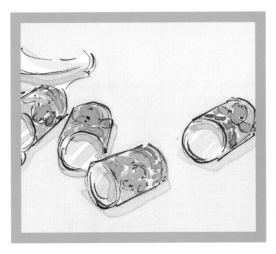

words by Jill McDougall
illustrated by Pat Reynolds

"I can push," said Ling.

She pushed and pushed.

"It will not go," said Ling.

4

"You are too little," said Mom.

"I can get the dog food,"
said Ling.

She jumped up.

The cans fell down.

"You are too little," said a man.

"I can take a bag," said Ling.

The cans fell out.

"You are too little," said Mom.

One can rolled away.

"I can not get it,"
said Mom.

"I can get it," said Ling.

"You are too big," said Ling.